In the M...

Poems chosen by
Richard Brown and Kate Ruttle

Illustrated by Irene Trivas

CAMBRIDGE
UNIVERSITY PRESS

Cambridge Reading

General Editors
Richard Brown and Kate Ruttle

Consultant Editor
Jean Glasberg

Published by the Press Syndicate of the University of Cambridge
The Pitt Building, Trumpington Street, Cambridge CB2 1RP
40 West 20th Street, New York, NY10011-4211, USA
10 Stamford Road, Oakleigh, Melbourne 3166, Australia

First published 1996

In The Mirror
This selection © Richard Brown and Kate Ruttle 1996
Illustrations © Irene Trivas 1996

Printed in Great Britain at the University Press, Cambridge

A catalogue record for this book is available from the British Library

ISBN 0 521 49997 6 paperback

Acknowledgements

We are grateful to the following for permission to reproduce copyright material:
'If I Could Only Take Home a Snowflake' by John Agard from *I Din do Nuttin*. The Bodley Head.
'Only the Lonely' by Tony Bradman from *Smile, Please!* Viking Kestrel Books, 1987. Copyright © Tony Bradman, 1987. Reproduced by permission of Penguin Books Ltd.
'New Shoes' © Richard Brown, 1996.
'Reflection' by Myra Cohn Livingston from *Wide Awake and Other Poems* by Myra Cohn Livingston. Copyright © Myra Cohn Livingston, 1959. Copyright renewed 1987 by Myra Cohn Livingston. Reprinted by permission of Marian Reiner for the author.
'Who Is It?' by Theresa Heine from *A Big Poetry Book*. Blackwell, 1989. Copyright © Theresa Heine, 1989.
'The Leader' by Roger McGough from *Sky in the Pie*. Penguin Books Ltd (Kestrel). Reprinted by permission of the Peters Fraser & Dunlop Group Ltd.
'The End' by A.A. Milne from *Now We Are Six* by A.A. Milne. Methuen Children's Books.
'Look-Alike' © Judith Nicholls, 1995. Reprinted by permission of the author.
'Stretching' by Hiawyn Oram from *Speaking For Ourselves*. Mammoth, 1992. Copyright © Hiawyn Oram, 1990. Reproduced by permission of the author c/o Rogers, Coleridge & White Ltd, 20 Powis Mews, London W11 1JN.
'Whistling' by Jack Prelutsky from *Here We Go*. HarperCollins Publishers, 1982.
'This Is the Hand' by Michael Rosen from *Is a Caterpillar Ticklish?* Puffin, Penguin Books. Reprinted by permission of the Peters Fraser & Dunlop Group Ltd.

Every effort has been made to reach copyright holders; the publishers would like to hear from anyone whose rights they have unknowingly infringed.

Contents

Reflection *Myra Cohn Livingston* 4
Who Is It? *Theresa Heine* 5
When I Was Small *Jay Reed* 6
Stretching *Hiawyn Oram* 7
This Is the Hand *Michael Rosen* 8
The End *A.A. Milne* 10
This Tooth *Lee Bennett Hopkins* 12
In My New Clothing *Basho* 13
New Shoes *Richard Brown* 14
Only the Lonely *Tony Bradman* 16
The Leader *Roger McGough* 17
Look-Alike *Judith Nicholls* 18
**If I Could Only Take Home
  a Snowflake** *John Agard* 20
Whistling *Jack Prelutsky* 22

Index of first lines 24

Reflection

In the mirror
I can see
Lots of things
But mostly – me.

Myra Cohn Livingston

Who Is It?

Take . . .
A head, some shoulders, knees, and toes,
A mouth and eyes that see,
A pair of legs, two feet, one nose,
And what you've got is
ME!

Theresa Heine

When I Was Small

When I was small
the wall was tall.
But now I'm tall
the wall looks small.

Jay Reed

Stretching

When I stretch
I'm ten foot tall
My legs can reach
Across the hall
My fingers grow
In leaps and bounds
My voice can make
The longest sounds
(AAAHHH AND EEEHHH
AND UHHHH AND URGHHHHH)
And when I stop
The stretching tall
It seems enormous
Being small

Hiawyn Oram

This Is the Hand

This is the hand
that touched the frost
that froze my tongue
and made it numb

This is the hand
that cracked the nut
that went in my mouth
and never came out

This is the hand
that slid round the bath
to find the soap
that wouldn't float

This is the hand
on the hot water bottle
meant to warm my bed
that got lost instead

This is the hand
that held the bottle
that let go of the soap
that cracked the nut
that touched the frost
this is the hand
that never gets lost.

Michael Rosen

The End

When I was One,
I had just begun.

When I was Two,
I was nearly new.

When I was Three,
I was hardly Me.

When I was Four,
I was not much more.

When I was Five,
I was just alive.

But now I am Six, I'm as clever as clever.
So I think I'll be six now for ever and ever.

A.A. Milne

This Tooth

I jiggled it
  jaggled it
    jerked it.

I pushed
  and pulled
    and poked it.

But –

As soon as I stopped,
and left it alone,
This tooth came out
on its very own!

Lee Bennett Hopkins

In My New Clothing

In my new clothing
I feel so different
I must
Look like someone else.

Basho

New Shoes

Each time
I slip on
a new pair of shoes
I'm a new person.

They change the way
I look.
They change the way
I feel.
They make me new, too.

My new shoes
and my old feet
take all day
to say hello.

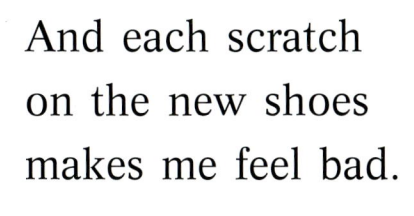

And each scratch
on the new shoes
makes me feel bad.

When do new shoes
become old shoes?
When we both
feel the same,
used to each other,
like friends.

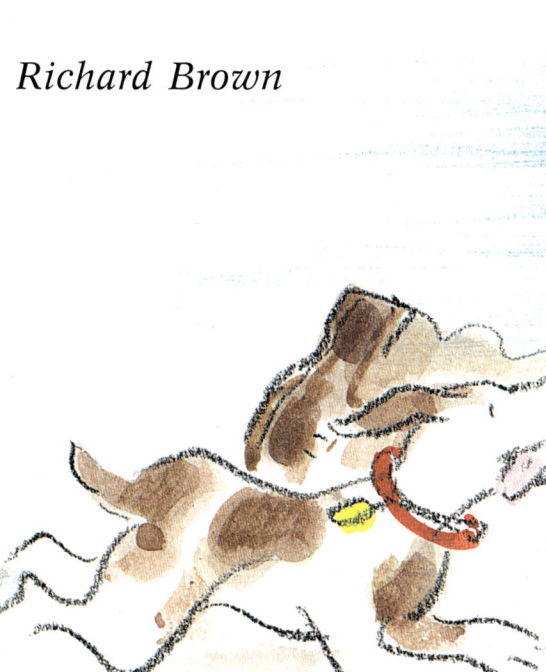

Richard Brown

Only the Lonely

I've never had
A room of my own
I've never been able
To sit alone
And read or think
Or laze about
Alone in the quiet

I'm only alone
When I go

Out

Tony Bradman

The Leader

I wanna be the leader
I wanna be the leader
Can I be the leader?
Can I? I can?
Promise? Promise?
Yippee, I'm the leader
I'm the leader

OK what shall we do?

Roger McGough

Look-Alike

I'm a . . .
look-alike
hair-alike
play-alike
share-alike

eat-alike
drink-alike
speak-alike
think-alike

sing-alike
scream-alike
laugh-alike
dream-alike

joke-alike
cook-alike
TALK-ALIKE

    L O O K - A L I K E

Me too!

I'm a . . .
look-alike
hair-alike
play-alike
share-alike

eat-alike
drink-alike
speak-alike
think-alike

sing-alike
scream-alike
laugh-alike
dream-alike

joke-alike
cook-alike
TALK-ALIKE

TWIN!

Me too!

Judith Nicholls

If I Could Only Take Home a Snowflake

Snowflakes
like tiny
insects
drifting
down.

Without a hum
they come,
Without a hum
they go.

Snowflakes
like tiny
insects
drifting
down.

If only
I could take
one
home with me
to show
my friends
in the sun,
just for fun,
just for fun.

John Agard

Whistling

Oh, I can laugh and I can sing
and I can scream and shout,
but when I try to whistle,
the whistle won't come out.

I shape my lips the proper way,
I make them small and round,
but when I blow, just air comes out,
there is no whistling sound.

But I'll keep trying very hard
to whistle loud and clear,
and some day soon I'll whistle tunes
for everyone to hear.

Jack Prelutsky

Index of first lines

Each time   14

I jiggled it   12

I wanna be the leader   17

I'm a . . .   18

I've never had   16

In my new clothing   13

In the mirror   4

Oh, I can laugh and I can sing   22

Snowflakes   20

Take . . .   5

This is the hand   8

When I stretch   7

When I was One   10

When I was small   6